CRISPR

and Other Biotech

World Book, Inc.
180 North LaSalle Street
Suite 900
Chicago, Illinois 60601
USA

For information about other "Cool Tech" titles, as well as other World Book print and digital publications, please go to www.worldbook.com.

For information about other World Book publications, call 1-800-WORLDBK (967-5325).

For information about sales to schools and libraries, call 1-800-975-3250 (United States) or 1-800-837-5365 (Canada).

Library of Congress Cataloging-in-Publication Data for this volume has been applied for.

Cool Tech
ISBN: 978-0-7166-2429-5 (set, hc.)

CRISPR and Other Biotech
ISBN: 978-0-7166-2434-9 (hc.)

Also available as:
ISBN: 978-0-7166-2451-6 (e-book)

Printed in China by RR Donnelley,
Guangdong Province
1st printing July 2019

STAFF

Editorial

Writer
Kris Fankhouser

Manager, New Content
Jeff De La Rosa

Manager, New Product
Development
Nick Kilzer

Proofreader
Nathalie Strassheim

Manager, Contracts and
Compliance
(Rights and Permissions)
Loranne K. Shields

Manager, Indexing Services
David Pofelski

Digital

Director, Digital Product
Development
Erika Meller

Digital Product Manager
Jonathan Wills

Graphics and Design

Senior Designer
Don DiSante

Media Editor
Rosalia Bledsoe

Manufacturing/ Production

Manufacturing Manager
Anne Fritzinger

Production Specialist
Curley Hunter

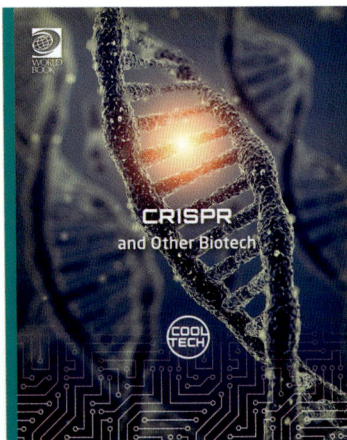

Credit: © No Beast So Fierce/Shutterstock

CONTENTS

INTRODUCTION

When an idea catches on quickly, it is often said to "go viral," multiplying and spreading like a living thing. **Biotechnology** is about to go viral—in more ways than one. Biotechnology—also called biotech—is the use of living things and life processes to benefit human beings.

Biotech may seem like a new idea, but people have been managing living things to their benefit for thousands of years. Perhaps the earliest biotech innovation was the domestication and breeding of plants and animals, at the very dawn of civilization. Some fairly complex biotechnology goes into the making of many everyday foods, such as cheese or beer.

But modern science has turned biotechnology up a notch. New techniques promise to revolutionize everything in our lives, from medicine to agriculture and everything in between. Biotechnology may even help humans to live longer.

In this book, you will read how biotechnology is being used today. You will learn about some of the latest advancements in medicine, agriculture, and other fields. You will also discover biotech advancements poised to go viral in the near future.

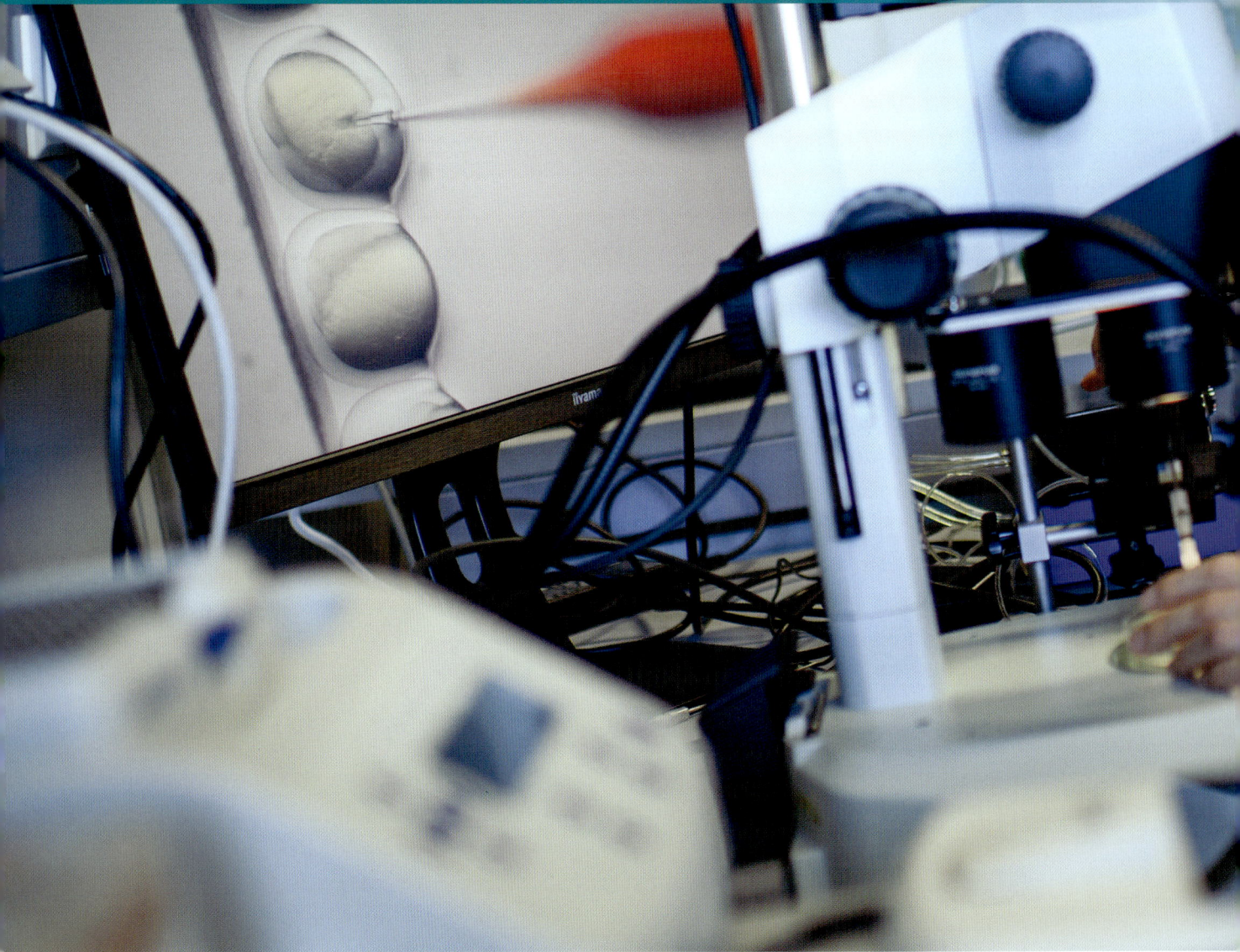

1 CRISPR

WHAT IS CRISPR?

CRISPR (pronounced "crisper") is a revolutionary technique in **genetic engineering.** Genetic engineering is the use of technology to alter a living thing's **genes**—the sequences of **DNA** that determine its characteristics. CRISPR can be used to "edit" DNA with extreme precision. By editing an organism's DNA, CRISPR can literally rewrite the code of life.

CRISPR stands for *C*lustered *R*egularly *I*nterspaced *S*hort *P*alindromic *R*epeats. The name refers to DNA sequences found in natural CRISPR systems. One common CRISPR system uses an *enzyme* called Cas9. An enzyme is a protein that speeds up or makes possible a chemical reaction in living things. CRISPR enzymes act like scissors, making cuts at precise locations in DNA molecules. These cuts trigger the cell's natural machinery to repair the DNA.

By manipulating this natural repair process, scientists use CRISPR to "cut and paste" the DNA, deleting, altering, or replacing a cell's genes with great accuracy. Because genes have a wide variety of functions, the changes that can be made using CRISPR are virtually limitless.

CRISPR enables genetic engineers to make cuts in the DNA molecule *(right),* deleting, altering, or replacing genes. The "edited" DNA can be injected into living cells, altering the characteristics of a living thing.

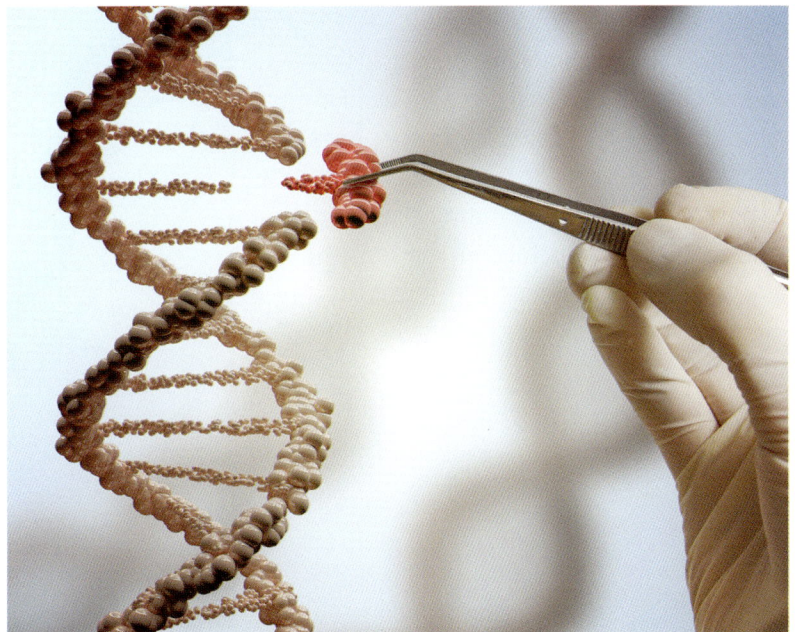

USES OF CRISPR

CRISPR technology has many potential uses. There are applications in medicine, agriculture, and energy production. Some applications of CRISPR technology are already underway, but others have yet to be developed. Soon, nearly every field of biotechnology will be transformed by CRISPR techniques.

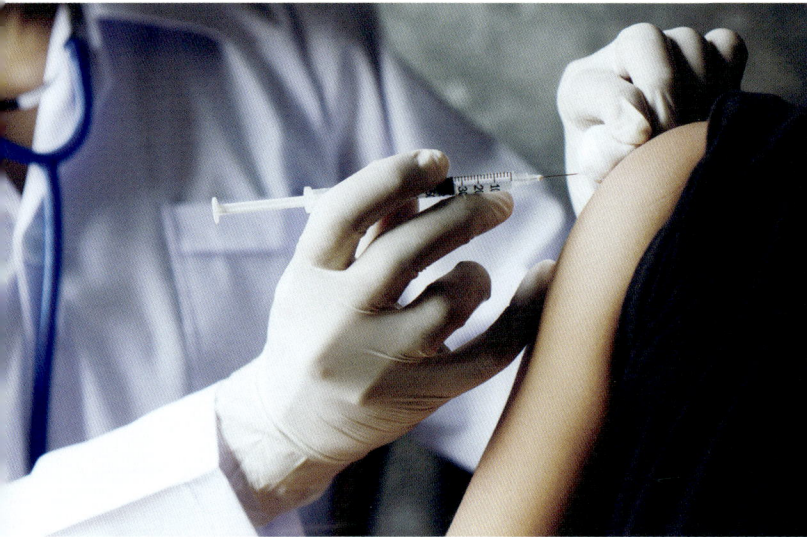

Biofuel. CRISPR may be helpful in the production of biofuel, a fuel produced directly from living matter. Scientists are using CRISPR techniques to genetically modify yeast cells used in the production of ethanol, a biofuel. They believe CRISPR can make biofuels more efficient and cheaper to produce.

Miracle cure? CRISPR has a huge number of potential uses in medicine. Researchers hope to use CRISPR to reprogram human immune cells to attack cancer cells. CRISPR may also be used in gene therapy, the transfer of new genes into a patient's cells to replace defective or missing genes. Gene therapy could lead to a cure for such genetic diseases as cystic fibrosis, hemophilia, muscular dystrophy, and sickle-cell anemia.

"Crisper" cabbage. Agricultural scientists are manipulating plant genes with CRISPR to create crops that grow more efficiently. Genetically engineered crops may require less water or resist plant diseases. CRISPR can also be used to grow crops that are more flavorful and stay fresh longer.

Healthier hogs. Scientists can use CRISPR to engineer animals with desirable traits and eliminate undesirable ones. Hogs and cattle can be altered to produce leaner, healthier meat in greater amounts using less feed.

GENE DRIVES

Genetic engineers have succeeded at changing living things in the laboratory. But for years, they have dreamed of making genetic changes that could spread in the wild. Imagine, for example, inserting a gene into a mosquito that prevented it from spreading the deadly disease malaria. If such a gene could be spread throughout the wild mosquito population, millions of lives would be saved each year. Such a possibility might be just around the corner, thanks to a technique called the *gene drive*.

Mosquitoes, like many other living things, reproduce sexually—that is, each mosquito offspring has a mother and a father. Every mosquito also has two copies of each gene, one from its mother and one from its father.

Now imagine creating a mosquito with two copies of the gene to prevent the transmission of malaria and releasing that mosquito into the wild. Each of the mosquito's offspring would have one copy of the new gene, and another, unaltered copy from its other parent. Each parent only passes on one copy of a gene to each offspring, more or less at random. So when the next generation of mosquitoes goes to reproduce, only about half the offspring will have the malaria-resistant gene. In the next generation, only one-quarter will have the new gene. It is easy to see how the new gene will have a tough time spreading in the wild.

That is where the gene drive comes. A gene drive embeds CRISPR technology in an engineered gene, enabling the gene to copy itself. With a gene drive, if a mosquito inherits one altered gene, that gene might overwrite the mosquito's unaltered copy, leading the mosquito to pass the altered gene to all its offspring. Over many generations, the new gene might spread throughout the mosquito population.

Gene drives are a powerful technology, with the potential to change entire population of living things. Many scientists caution against the use of gene drives until the dangers are more fully understood.

Scientists are experimenting with gene drives that could make wild mosquitoes unable to carry the **parasite** that causes malaria. A scientist uses a microscope and fine syringe to inject CRISPR-altered DNA in mosquito embryos *(opposite)*.

THE FUTURE OF CRISPR

The possibilities of CRISPR seem limitless. With this powerful and precise gene-editing technology, scientists believe they can cure even grow **organs** for tranplant, eliminate hunger, and bring animals back from extinction.

Growing organs for transplant. Medical researchers are investigating the use of CRISPR to genetically alter pigs, enabling them to grow organs suitable for **transplant** to humans.

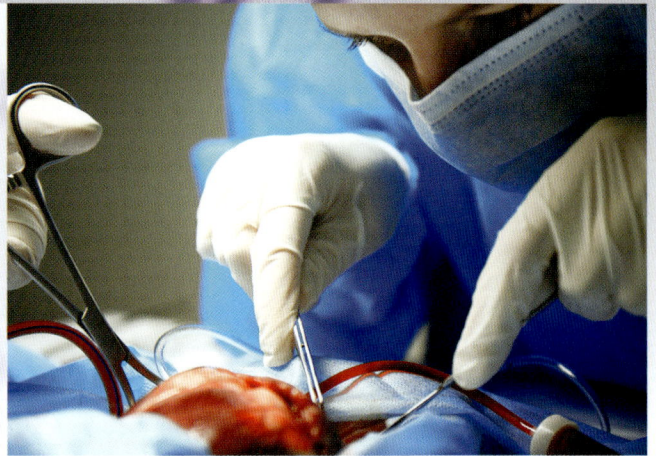

Feeding a hungry world. There are many places in the world where people face food shortages, but CRISPR could soon change all that. For example, scientists at Cold Spring Harbor Laboratory in New York have used CRISPR technology to improve the yield of tomato plants. If this method is applied to other crops, CRISPR could help to eliminate widespread hunger and malnutrition.

Bringing back the dead. CRISPR could be used to bring back living things that have gone **extinct.** Researchers at Harvard University announced that they were using CRISPR technology to help test woolly mammoth cells, in hopes that they can bring this species back from extinction. If this experiment is successful, other extinct species could be revived as well.

JURASSIC PARK

In the science-fiction novel *Jurassic Park* (1990) by Michael Crichton (later made into a popular film series), dinosaurs are brought back to life and cause widespread destruction. Some scientists have urged caution in the use of CRISPR technology. If it is not handled carefully, *Jurassic Park*-style disasters may no longer be the stuff of science fiction.

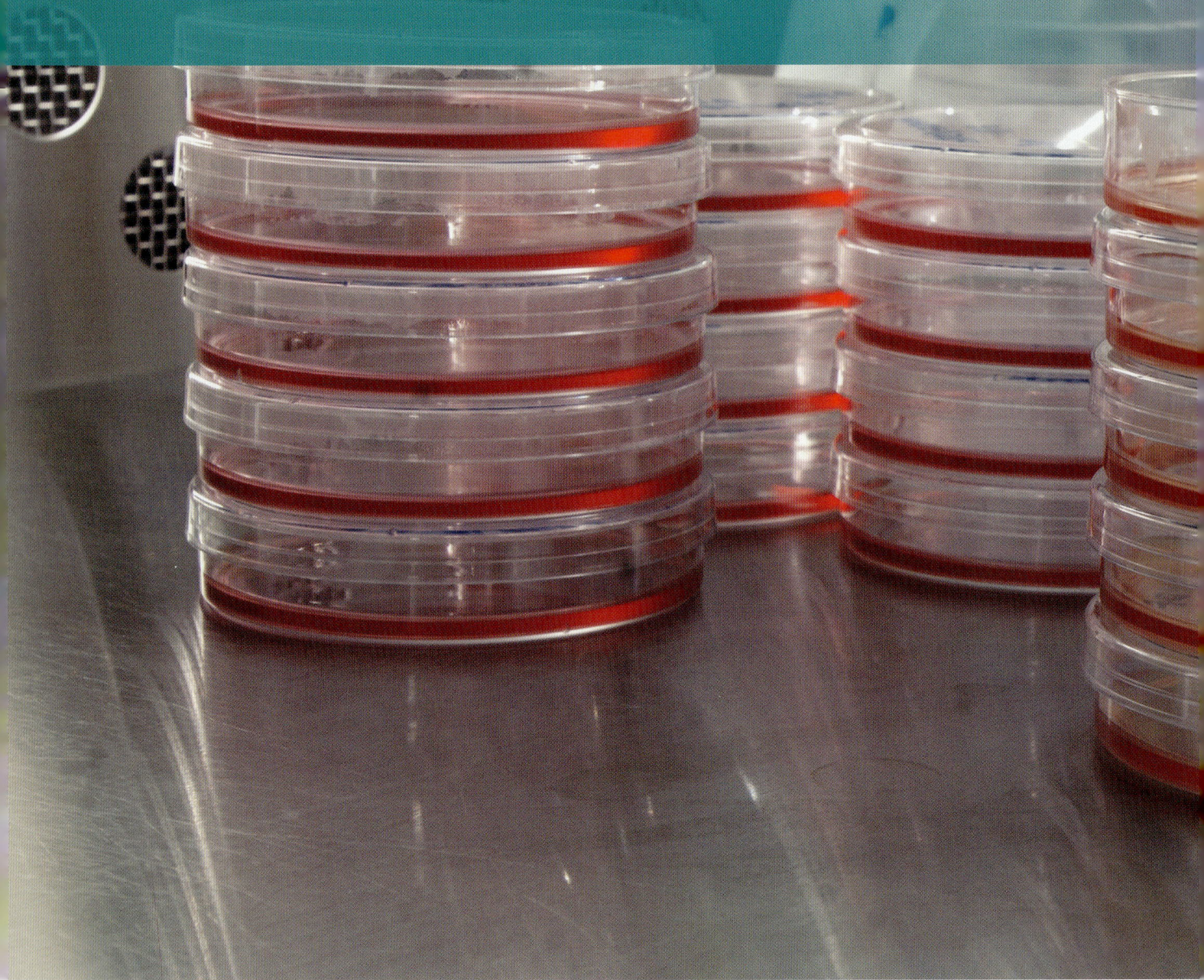

2 STEM CELLS

CREATING NEW CELLS

Stem cells are another cool biotechnology ready to change the future of medicine. A stem cell is a cell with the ability to produce more stem cells or, more importantly, other types of cells, such as blood or nerve cells. The original cells from which a tiny embryo develops into a person are stem cells.

Adults have stem cells, too. They help keep us healthy. Think of these adult stem cells as live-in repair personnel that can fix most anything. The reserve supply of cells can be used when the body starts to break down and needs repair.

Stem cells are found in many places in the adult body, including the skin, liver, bone marrow, and muscles. These stem cells remain inactive until they are needed. The stem cells supply each organ or tissue with the cells needed to replace damaged or dead cells. Some stem cells in the bone marrow may produce new bone and cartilage cells when needed.

Scientists are finding new ways to grow and use stem cells to improve health. Some stem cell biotechnology in the future may even help regenerate entire limbs.

Stem cells can transform into any other kind of cell in the body, including skin, liver, blood, muscle, and even nerve cells *(right)*. Stem cells cultured in the laboratory may be used to replace damaged cells in the body, revolutionizing medical treatment.

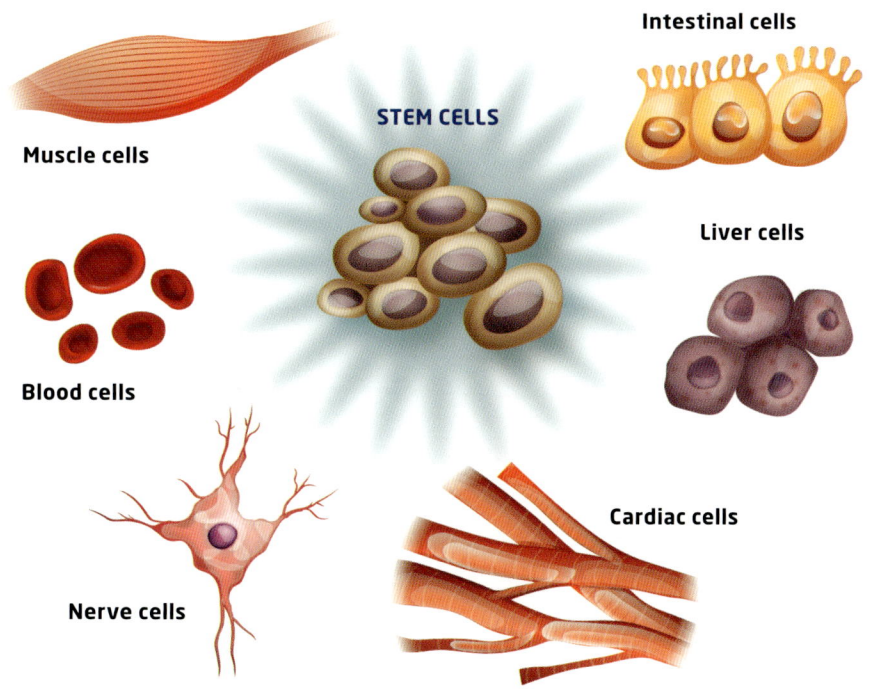

Muscle cells

Blood cells

Nerve cells

STEM CELLS

Intestinal cells

Liver cells

Cardiac cells

STEM CELL THERAPIES

Stem cell technology is still in its infancy. But it is developing quickly. Medical researchers are already using stem cell therapies to heal patients. As these techniques improve, scientists believe they can add many healthy years to a person's life.

Paralyzed no more. When the body is injured, the damaged tissues naturally repair themselves using stem cells. Scientists can now use these same cells to repair parts of the body that cannot repair themselves, such as nerves. Doctors have injected stem cells into the damaged spine of a paralyzed man. Months later, he showed improvement in sensation and movement in his limbs. Medical researchers hope that stem cells can one day cure paralysis.

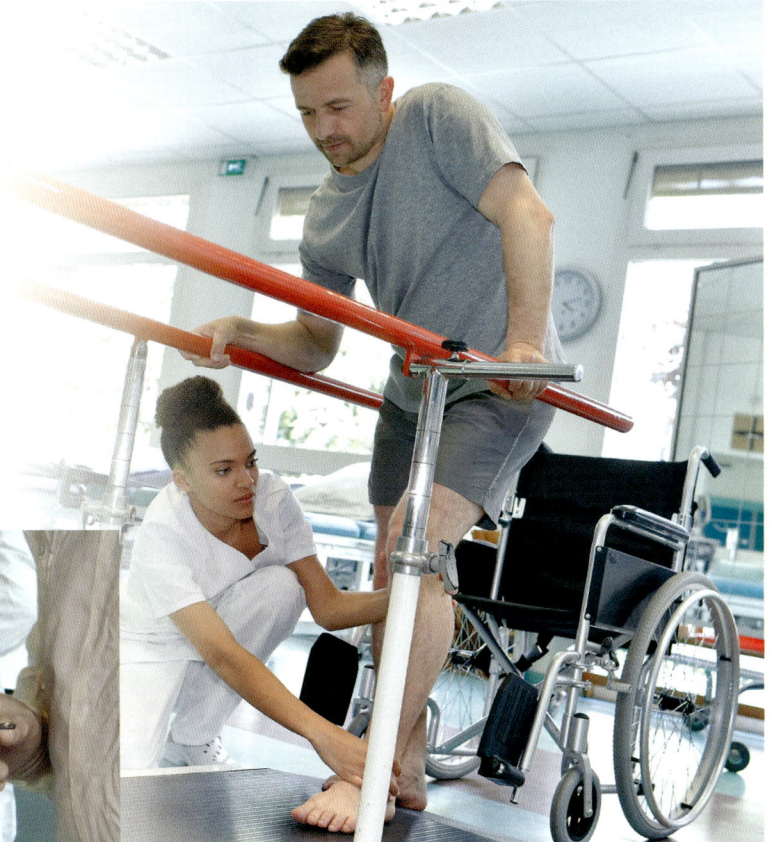

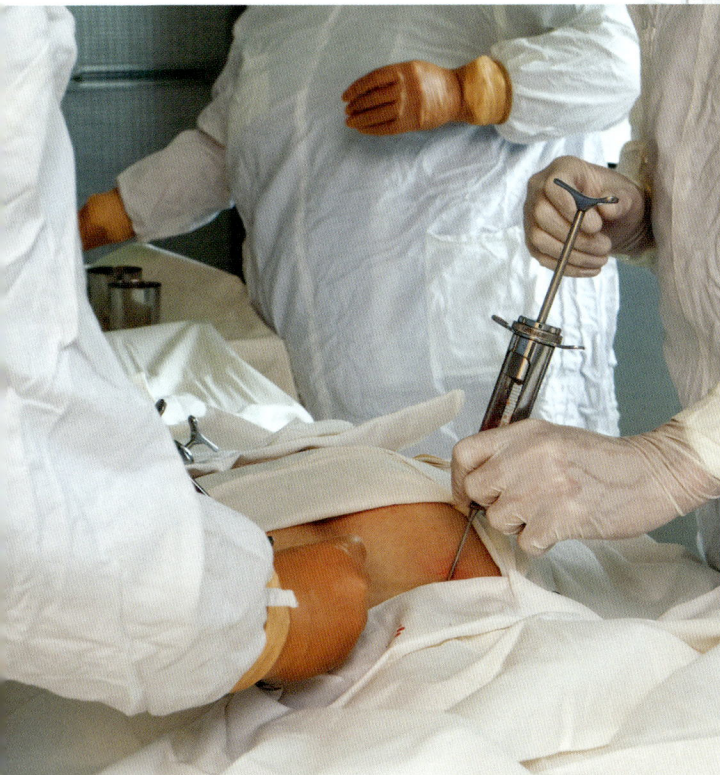

Stem cell transplants. Bone marrow transplants are the most common type of stem cell therapy. But scientists are looking into the possibility of using stem cells to treat a long list of diseases. They include cancer, diabetes, and heart disease and even conditions that involve nerve damage, such as Alzheimer's, Parkinsons and Lou Gehrig's disease.

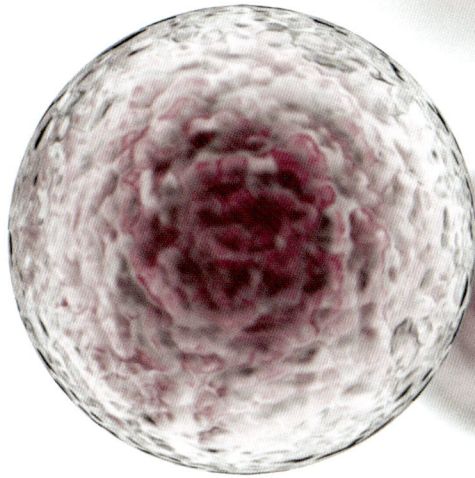

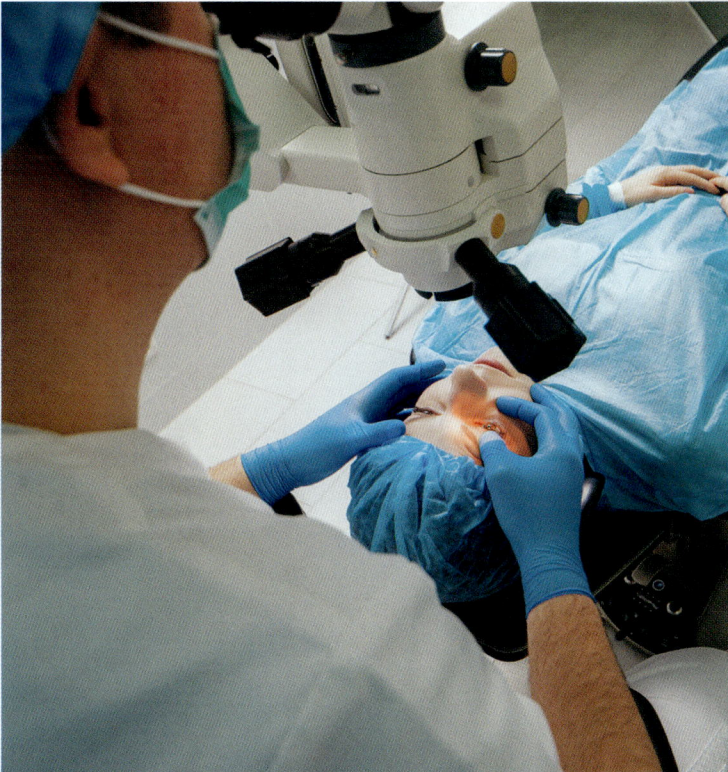

Restoring vision. Stem cells may be used to restore sight to the blind. With stem cells, scientists are able to grow retinas, corneas, and lenses that can be transplanted directly into a patient's eyes to restore sight.

THE FUTURE OF STEM CELLS

In the future, stem cells will be used for more than just bone marrow transplants. They may be used to build custom-fitted tisues and organs from scratch. People may keep their own supply of stem cells in biotechnology banks for safekeeping, in case of future need.

Tissue engineering. An increasing number of people suffer from diseased or damaged organs. Unfortunately, there is also a shortage of organ **donors.** Stem cell research may solve this problem through tissue engineering. Tissue engineering involves using the body's own stem cells to restore, replace, or improve diseased tissue. Scientists in the future may be able to use stem cells to produce made-to-order replacements for skin, bone, cartilage, and other organs and tissues that patients need.

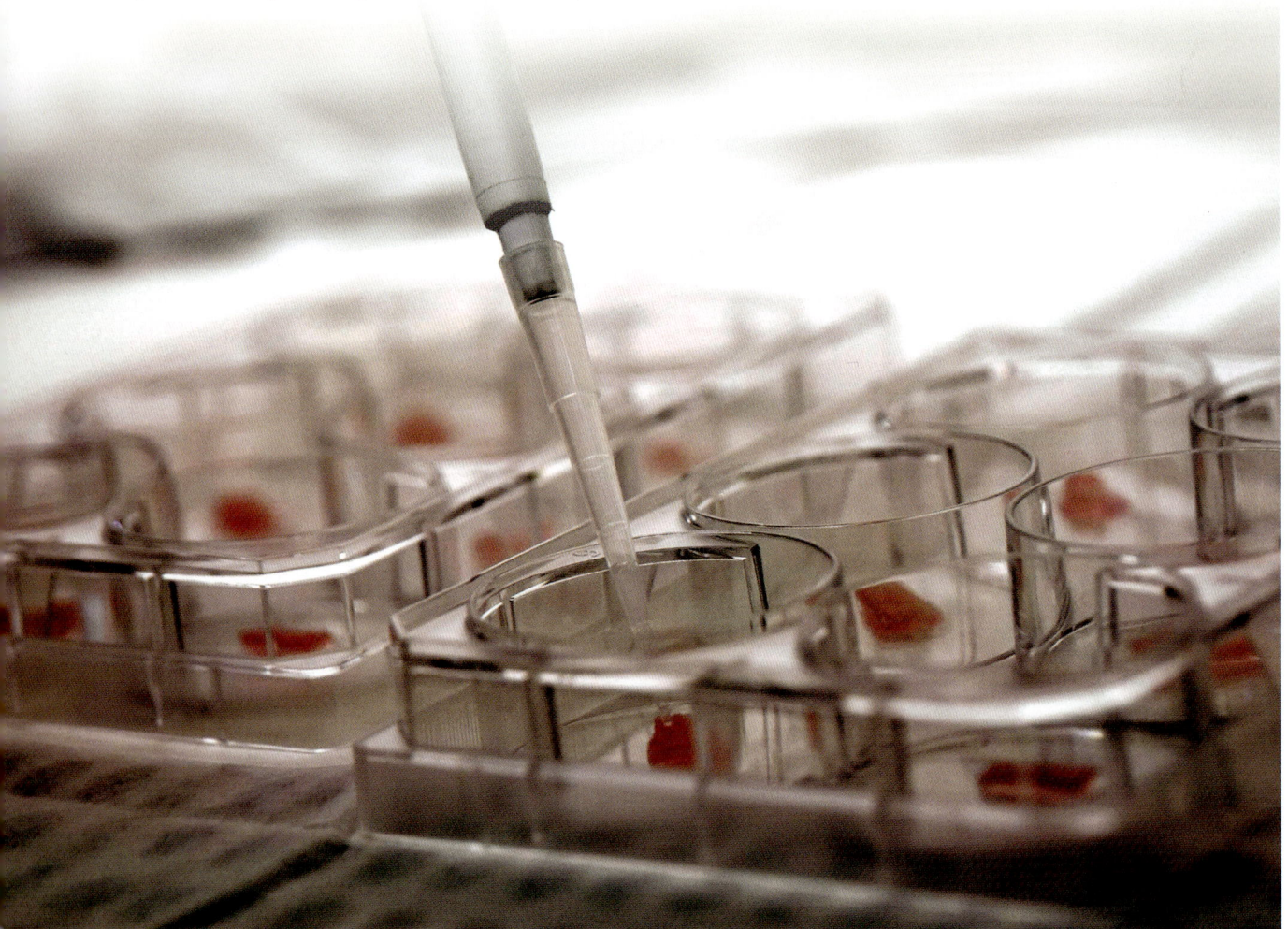

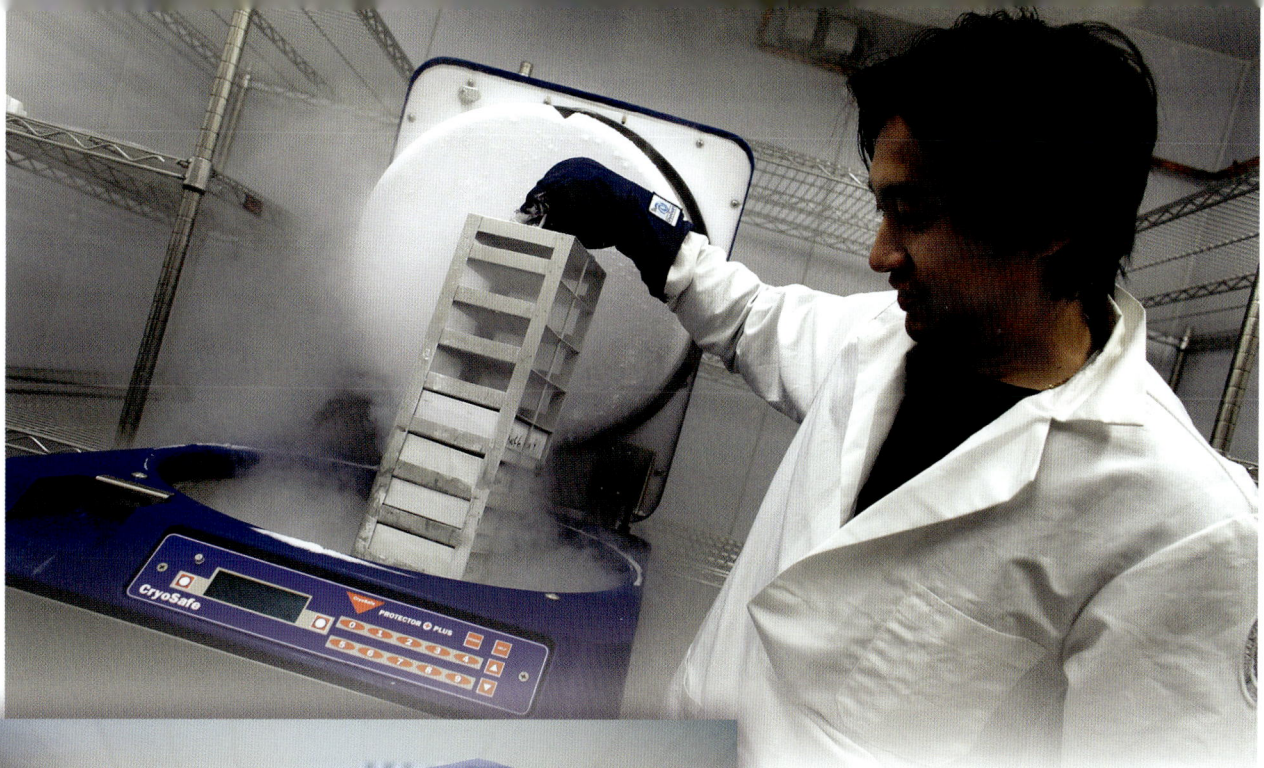

Stem cell banking. Just as blood banks store lifesaving blood for future use, stem cell banks may store stem cells. In the future, people may make a small "deposit" of stem cells shortly after birth. These cells can be copied and then frozen in storage, until they are needed. Scientists are looking into stem cell banks with great "interest."

Parabiosis is a controversial process that involves revitalizing an aging body with transfusions of blood from younger individuals. Some scientists suggest that regular infusions of "young" blood produced from stem cells into the body over time could increase both a person's health and lifespan.

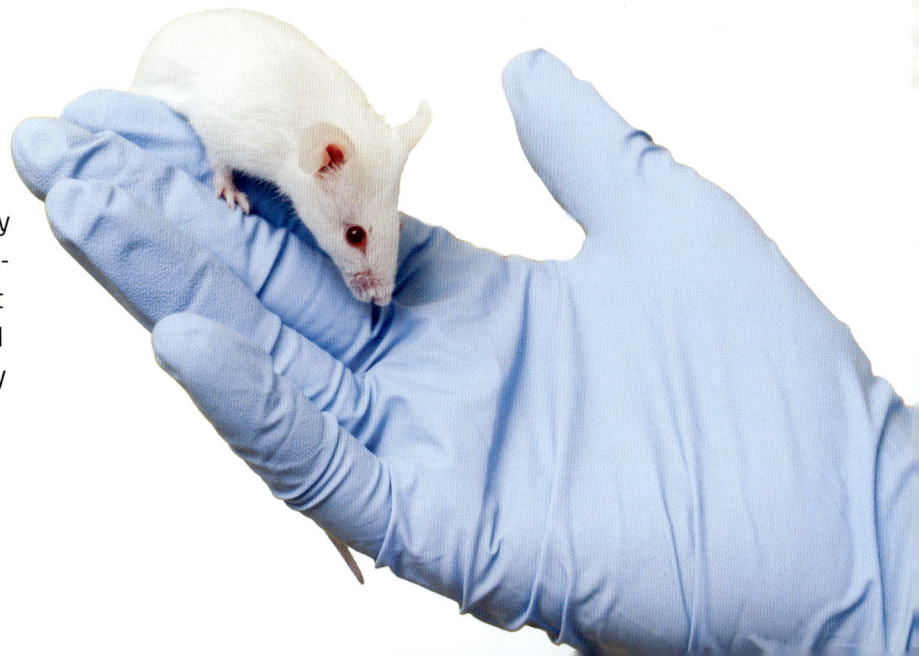

3 EXTENDING LIFE

Many cultures believe that they have discovered the secret to combating aging. A Chinese man practices the ancient art of Tai Chi *(right)*. A Scandinavian man immerses himself in cold water *(opposite)*.

THE FOUNTAIN OF YOUTH

Aging—everyone talks about it, but nobody does anything about it. Humans have always dreamed of immortality and eternal youth—the possibility of extending life. The myth of a Fountain of Youth, a magical spring that restores youth to those who drink or bathe in its waters, dates to ancient times. According to a popular legend, the Spanish explorer Ponce de León came to Florida in 1512 to find the Fountain of Youth. Old stories said that the waters of the spring were supposed to restore youth and cure sickness.

Today, that dream of extending life may now be within reach, thanks to biotechnology. Researchers in the field of life extension are working to increase the human life span with biotech. Some believe that living to the age of 125 years—and enjoying good health throughout life—will soon be possible for every human being.

MODERN RESEARCH

Anti-aging fads come and go. Most are untested and probably about as helpful as snake oil. Some may even be dangerous. Few experts think that aging can actually be reversed. Yet, as scientists better understand the biology of aging, they are discovering new ways to combat the ravages of time and help people live longer, more active lives.

Caloric restriction. Today, much of the research on extending life focuses on nutrition. Scientists noted that eating an extremely low-**calorie** diet seemed to increase the lifespan of mice and monkeys. They do not yet fully understand this process and do not know if it works in humans—so don't starve yourself! But, through biotechnology, scientists think they can create drugs that mimic the effects of these low-calorie diets. Then you can have your cake and eat it, too.

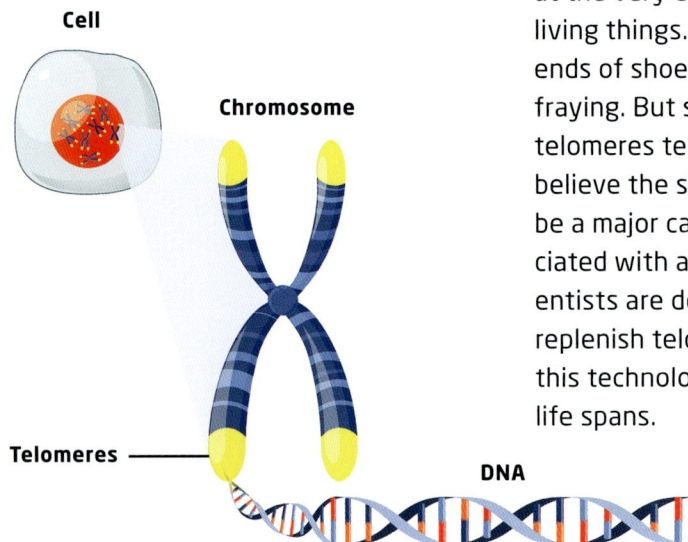

Telomeres are the protective structures at the very ends of **chromosomes** in most living things. The are a bit like the plastic ends of shoelaces that keep them from fraying. But scientists have observed that telomeres tend to shorten with age. They believe the shortening of telomeres may be a major cause of certain illnesses associated with aging. Using biotechnology, scientists are developing ways to artificially replenish telomeres. Scientists think that this technology may help extend healthy life spans.

Cell

Chromosome

Telomeres

DNA

People in different areas of the world have different life expectancies. People in Sardinia, Italy *(right)*, and Okinawa, Japan *(below)*, live longer than others. Do their lifestyles offer a secret to extending life?

"Curing" old age? Some experts in the medical field do not agree with the idea that the aging process is a disease that needs to be cured. They claim that aging is a natural and unavoidable part of life and that extending life indefinitely is simply not possible. They do not recognize the benefit of anti-aging medicine. Scientists also warns that many so-called anti-aging products available today have yet to be fully tested to determine if they are safe or—perhaps more importantly—effective.

INTO THE FUTURE

Some ideas about using biotechnology to extend life are a bit more far-fetched than others. They may seem better suited to science fiction, but they could be part of our biotech future.

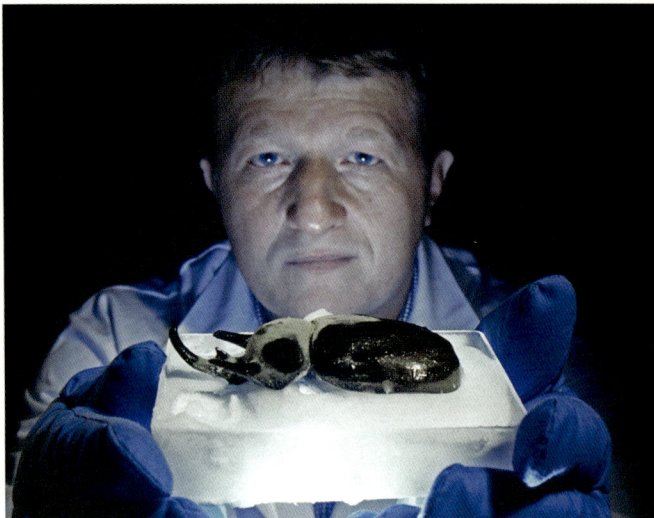

Cryonics revisited. The idea of cryonics—preserving bodies by freezing them for future revival—has been around since the 1950's. But new biotech methods for freezing and preserving bodies after death may make it a viable method to extend human life. Many animals—including beetles—can be frozen and revived upon thawing. Scientists who were once skeptical of cryonics are now starting to thaw to the idea.

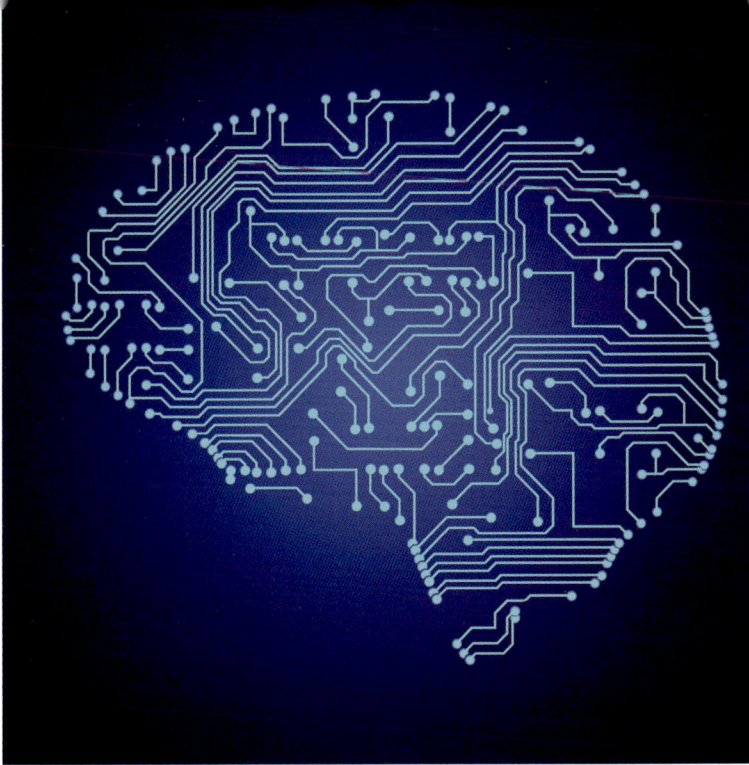

Mind uploading. One futuristic strategy to extend life involves uploading the mind into a computer. Some **futurists** claim that technology to "upload" human brains to computers could be available by the end of the century.

Cyborg—short for *cybernetic organism*—is a person who has some bodily functions performed by machines. In 2011, a company called Initiative 2045 was formed with the goal of designing real-life cyborgs. They hope to design an artificial body known as an **avatar** that can be controlled directly by a human brain.

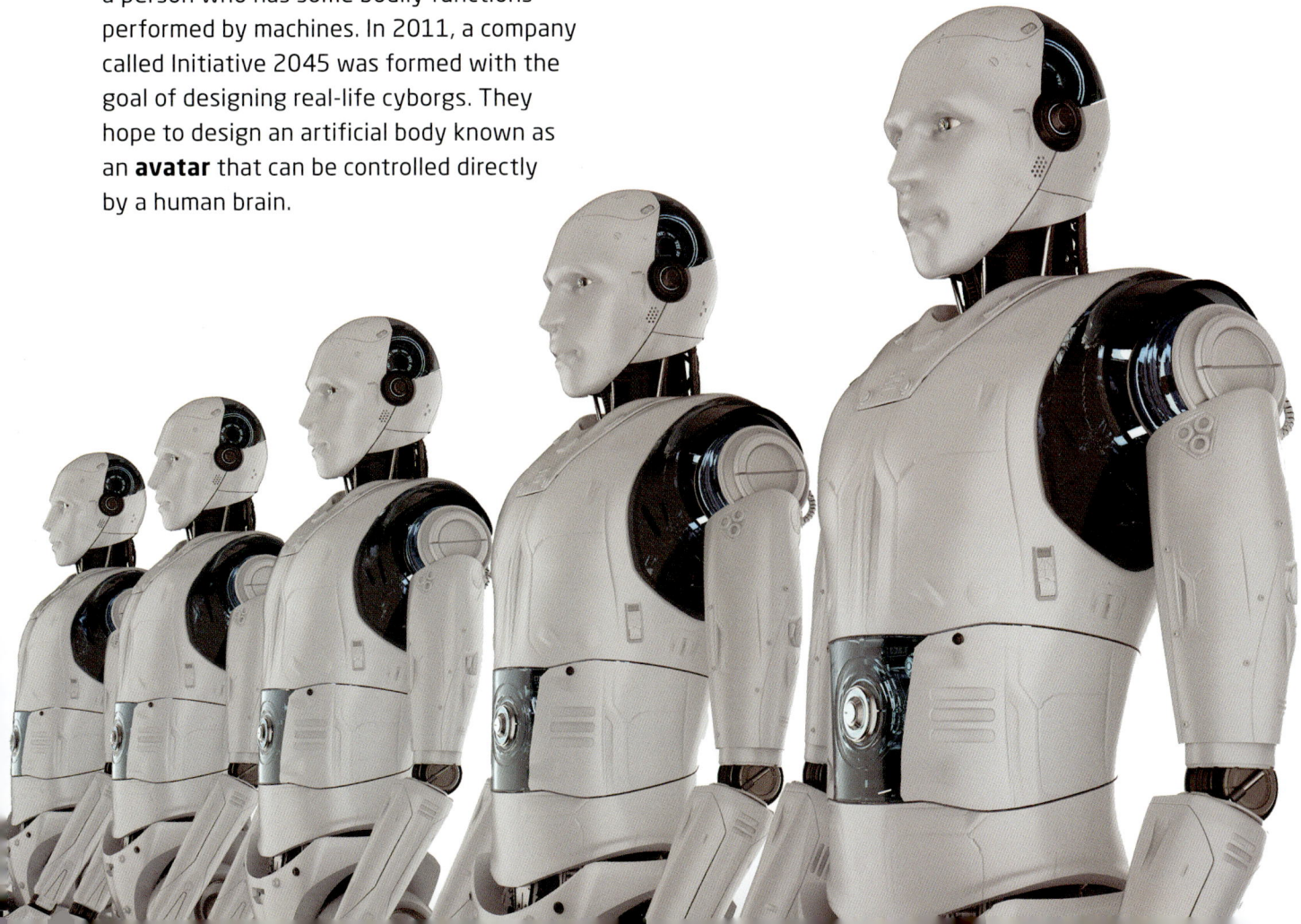

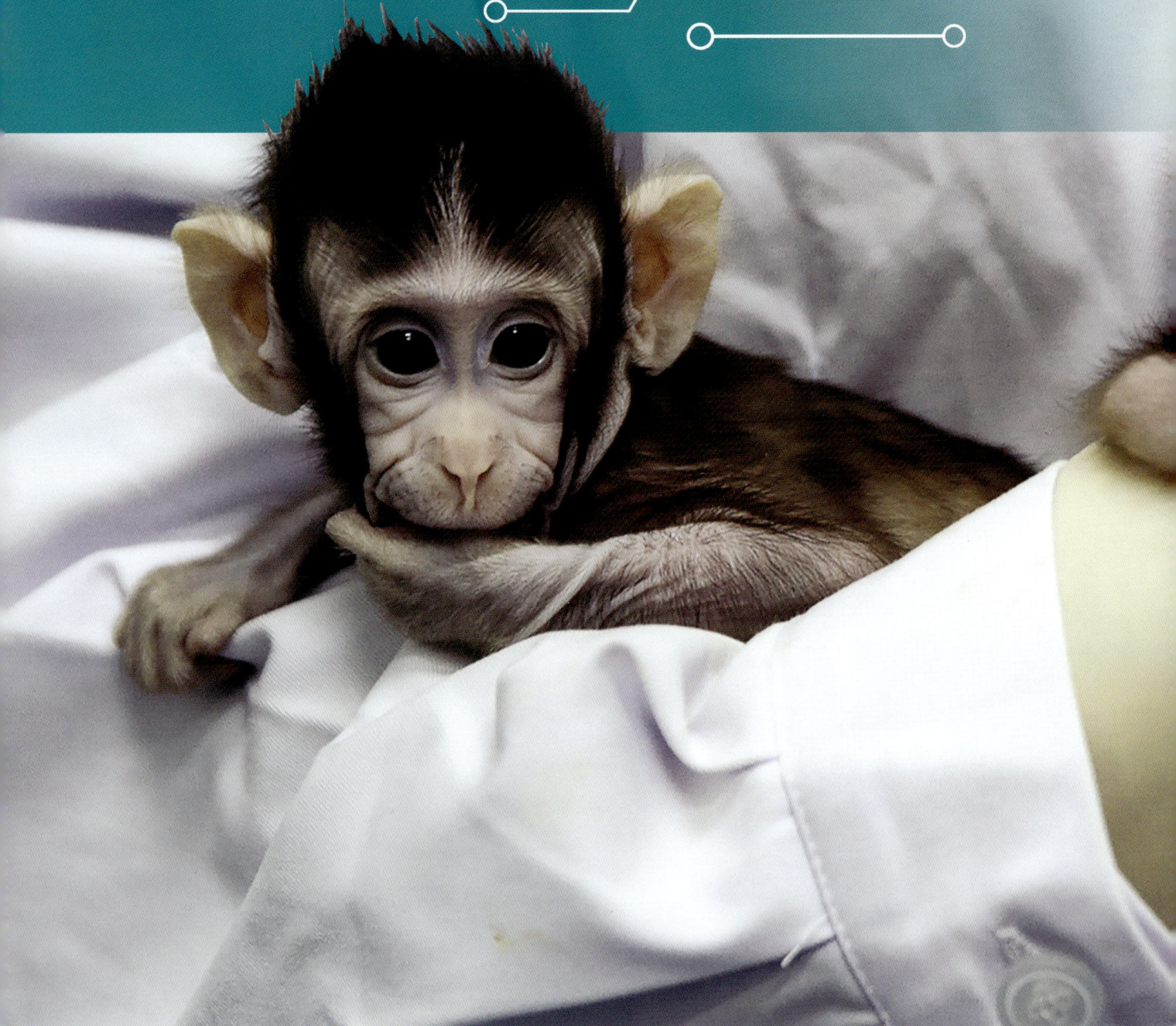

4 CLONING

YOU SEEM FAMILIAR

The promise of cloning in our biotech future has scientists beside themselves with excitement. Cloning is the creation of an organism with genetic material identical to that of another organism. Organisms that share an identical genetic makeup are called *clones.* Clones may look exactly alike.

Many examples of clones exist in nature. Identical twins are genetically exactly alike—they are natural clones. Most every cell in your body contains all of the necessary genetic information to create the entire new organism. This fact enables scientists to clone an entire animal from a single cell.

However, the purpose of most cloning research today is not to produce an unlimited number of identical people. Experiments with cloning and cloned animals have provided scientists with a great deal of information on biological processes. This information can be used to develop treatments for a wide variety of diseases and conditions, including cancer and birth defects. This kind of cloning is known as *therapeutic cloning.* Doctors might be able to use stem cells cloned from a patient to replace damaged tissues and treat diseases. Many scientists think the use of therapeutic cloning to make body tissues for transplant—such as skin, liver, and pancreas tissue—could revolutionize medicine.

But many people worry that cloning procedures may be used unethically. They could be used to reproduce people.

Clones of the same macaque appear in this photograph released by Chinese researchers. Clones are genetically identical to one another and may appear the same.

CLONING AND CONTROVERSY

Like many other developing fields in biotechnology, cloning is not without controversy. Scientists have found it difficult to consistently produce healthy animal clones. Most cloned embryos do not survive to reach birth. Some cloned animals that are born suffer developmental problems and die soon after birth. Cloning technology raises many questions about ethical issues and even safety. Many countries have enacted bans that limit cloning research.

Nuclear transfer is the process used to create clones. In this process, scientists remove the *nucleus* (center) of an adult body cell—which contains all its genes—and transfer it to an egg that has had its nucleus removed. The resulting cell can develop into a fully formed individual.

Biotech scientists imagine many uses for cloning. These include improvements to livestock and new medical therapies, including new drugs for human diseases, treatments for genetic disorders, and the possibility of transplanting modified organs from animals to humans.

Well, hello, Dolly! In 1996, a group led by the British scientist Ian Wilmut made a breakthrough that transformed the science of cloning. They succeeded in using nuclear transfer to clone a mammal. The clone, a sheep named Dolly, captured the world's imagination. But Dolly died in 2003 at age six— young for a sheep.

Food from clones. In 2008, officials at the United States Food and Drug Administration (FDA) announced that the meat and milk of such cloned animals as cows, goats, and pigs was as safe as that of noncloned animals. Consumer groups worry that the risks of widespread animal cloning are not fully known.

Human cloning. Scientists may soon use cloning techniques to reproduce human beings—a frightening prospect to many people. Today, virtually all cloning researchers reject the use of cloning to reproduce people. They cite the high incidence of abnormalities in cloned animals, along with other ethical concerns.

BREAKTHROUGHS IN CLONING

Many species of animal have been cloned since Dolly the sheep in 1996. These include cows, horses, pigs, rabbits, wolves, and others. In 2001, a *gaur* (also known as an Indian bison) became the first **endangered species** to be cloned.

Cloned animals have the same genes and may appear identical. A researcher holds cloned rabbits *(right)*.

Cloned pets. In 2004, a company named Genetic Savings & Clone, Inc., opened in California. They offered pet-cloning services to customers. That same year, a woman in Texas provided genetic material from her beloved pet cat, named Nicky, and paid $50,000 to have it cloned. The clone, known as Little Nicky *(below),* was the first cat to be cloned for commercial purposes.

The first cloned primates. In 1999, a rhesus monkey named Tetra was cloned using a process called embryo splitting. The cloning took place at the Oregon National Primate Research Center. Tetra was the first primate to be cloned. Primates are the group of mammals that includes monkeys, apes, and human beings.

Saved from extinction? The goatlike bucardo, or Pyrenean ibex, became extinct in 2000. But in 2003, a Spanish biotechnology company created a clone from frozen skin cells, marking the first extinct species to be brought back to life. This effort to save a species from extinction was ultimately unsuccessful, but scientists expect to make similar attempts in the future.

Man's best friend. In 2005, the first dog was cloned by researchers at Seoul National University in South Korea. An Afghan hound named Snuppy, it was produced by using cells from the ear of an adult Afghan hound. *Time* magazine named Snuppy the year's Most Amazing Invention in 2005.

5 THE HEALTHCARE OF TOMORROW

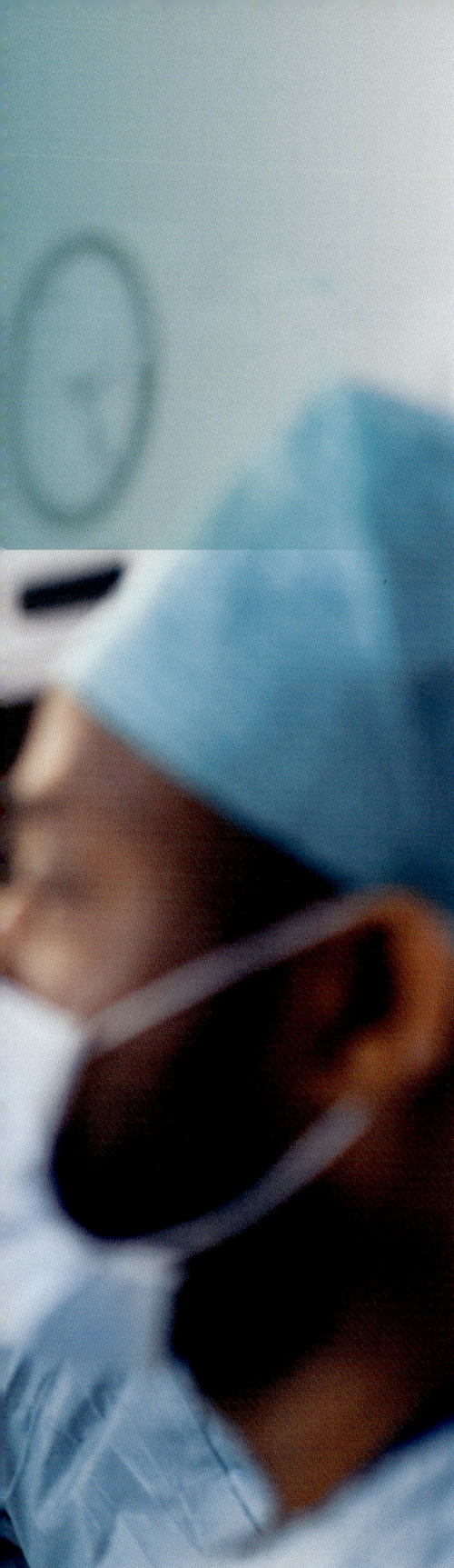

A BRAVE NEW WORLD

Technology is all about improving the human condition and the determination to make the world a better place. Nowhere is technology making more of an impact than in healthcare. Cutting-edge technology is already being used to improve health and quality of life for millions of people worldwide. Cool new biotech trends mean the future will be even more awesome.

Innovation in technology and healthcare often go hand-in-hand. Almost any advancement in technology has immediate applications to medicine and healthcare fields. These include advancements in biotechnology, of course, but also in such varied fields as communications, computer technology, materials science, and even robotics.

New technologies do not always deliver on their promise, however. Advances in medical technology are often expensive and available to few patients. To truly change the world, technological advances must deliver vital health services to all the people who need them while keeping costs as low as possible. New technologies can help here, too. Telemedicine and artificial intelligence can help healthcare providers see more patients and more quickly make diagnoses and treatment plans. With proper planning and care, the new technologies of healthcare can improve the quality of life for all.

MED TECH

Technology is transforming the practice of medicine. One area of rapid development is telemedicine, the use of communications technology to connect doctors and patients at a distance. Robots and artificial intelligence are also poised to extend the healing powers of medical professionals.

Telemedicine is already allowing doctors to examine and diagnose patients remotely, through online videoconferencing. Telemedicine enables patients to waste less time in the waiting room and to get immediate care when they need it. Patients can access healthcare 24 hours a day, and doctors can monitor their patient's health with fitness trackers and other mobile apps and devices, actively managing their health.

WATSON

In 2011, an IBM supercomputer nicknamed Watson became world-famous by defeating two human contestants on the television game show "Jeopardy!" Watson went on to work in medicine. The computer now assists physicians and nurses in the treatment of cancer and other diseases.

Artificial intelligence (AI) is the ability of certain computer systems to process information in a manner similar to human thought or to exhibit human-like behavior. AI is already being used in medicine, where it assists radiologists in the detection and diagnosis of disease. More AI applications are being developed for medicine everyday. In the future, your next doctor appointment may be with a computer.

Rehab robots. Every year, millions of people suffer from strokes or other injuries that require medical **rehabilitation** to restore function. This process is being revolutionized by medical robots that can assist patients in physical therapy to regain strength and range of motion. Robots can assist patients to stand, find their balance, and learn to walk again. Some robots can even allow patients to rehabilitate in the comfort of their own home.

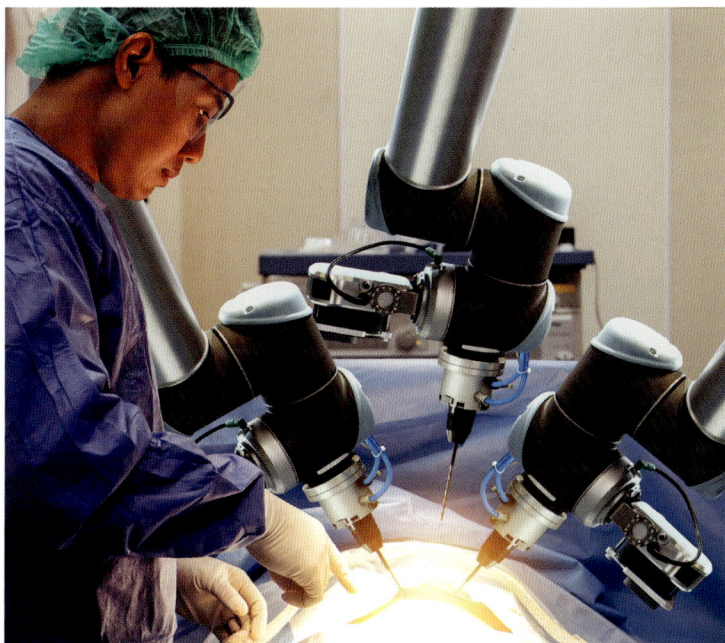

Robot surgery. Sophisticated robots can perform delicate operations better than the most steady-handed surgeons. But don't worry—the surgical robot is not actually conducting the operation. Instead, a surgeon provides instructions that the robot carries out. Tiny digital cameras allow the surgeon to see the operation up close. Your surgeon may not even be in the same room. Using robotic tools, surgeons can work inside the body through tiny incisions, much too small for human hands, and perform delicate operations with greater precision. The result is faster healing and recovery.

SPARE PARTS

Is your body feeling tired and worn out? Technology may soon be able to replace your worn-out parts. Robotic technology, for example, could provide an unlimited supply of spare limbs for the human body. Technology can already replace the human heart, and the list of body parts that doctors can switch out for mechanical substitutes continues to grow.

Prosthetics is the branch of medicine that deals with supplying artificial parts for the body. An artificial part, called a *prosthesis,* replaces a body part lost as the result of injury, disease, or defect. In 2013, scientists produced the first robotic arm that could read signals from the brain and be permanently attached to a person's body. Soon afterward, the first brain-controlled robotic leg was developed.

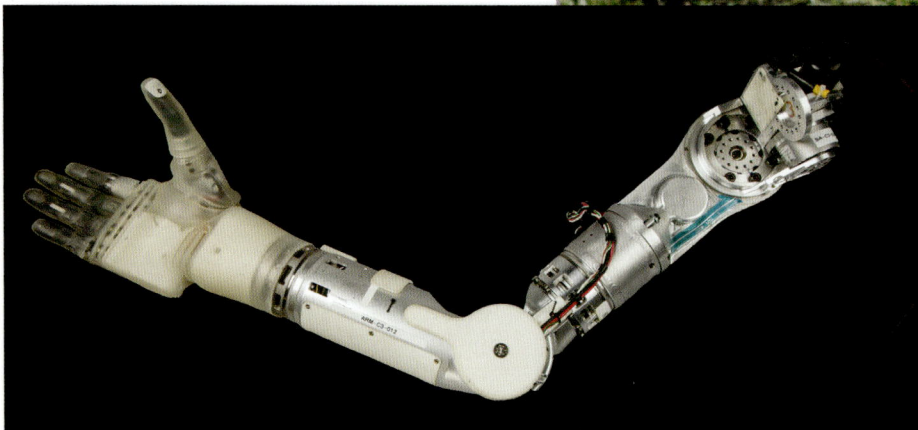

Artificial organs. In the 1980's, a team led by the American scientist Robert Jarvik designed an artificial heart. This device, known as the Jarvik-7, was successfully implanted into a human patient. Since then, many artificial **organs** have been successfully implanted, including the bladder, the liver, and the pancreas.

An artificial pancreas *(top right)* produces the hormone insulin for a woman with the disease diabetes.

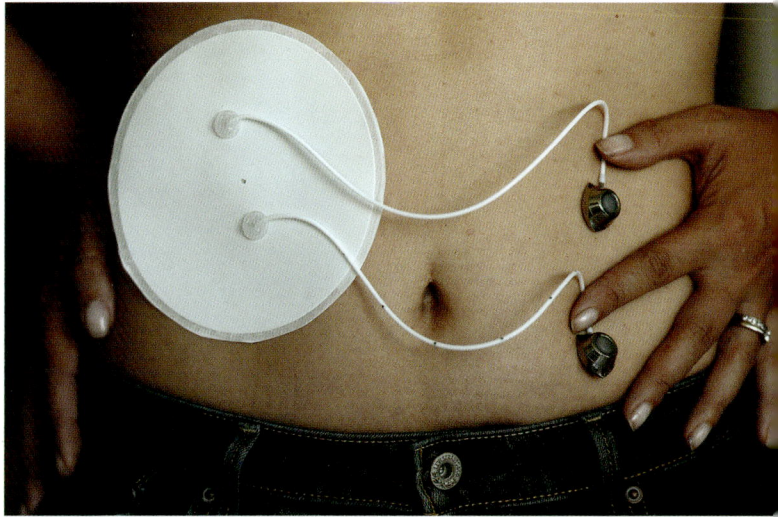

THE SIX MILLION DOLLAR MAN

In the 1970's, the television series "The Six Million Dollar Man" (based on the novel *Cyborg* by Martin Caidin) featured a character named Steve Austin, an astronaut whose right arm and legs were lost in a plane crash. They were replaced with high-tech **bionic** limbs that gave him extraordinary powers. The show was far-fetched science fiction at the time, but it now seems much closer to reality.

SCI-FI MEDICINE

The practice of medicine is increasingly starting to resemble science fiction. Engineers are developing sophisticated devices to diagnose illness and virtual reality systems to help patients and doctors.

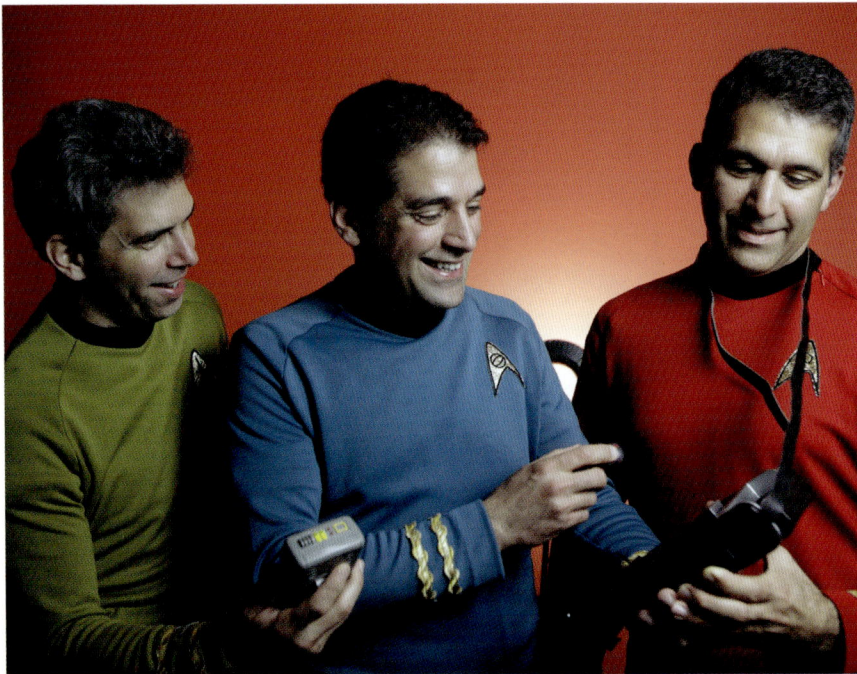

The inventors *(left)* of the experimental diagnostic technology DxtER drew inspiration from a device called a *tricorder,* used in the science fiction television series "Star Trek" (1966-1969).

DxtER, pronounced "Dexter," is an experimental device straight out of science fiction. It was developed in 2017 by a self-funded group of techies in Pennsylvania, led by an emergency medicine physician. DxtER makes use of an iPad to guide a patient through a series of tests that can help diagnose up to 34 common medical conditions.

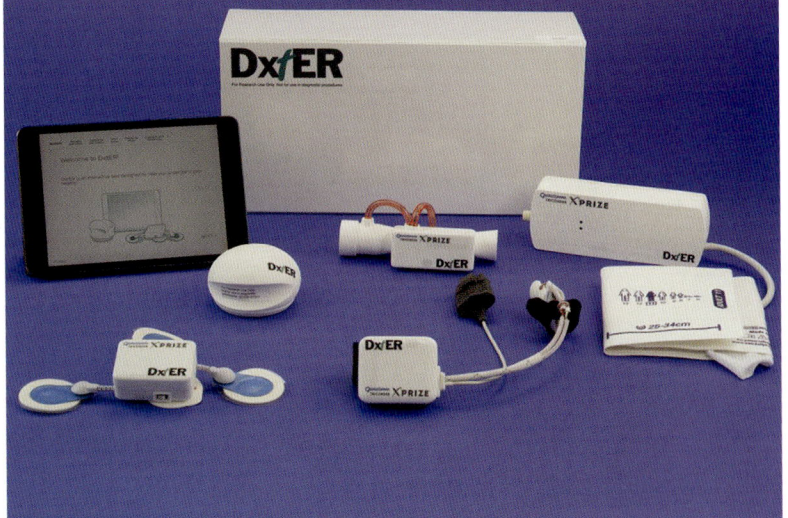

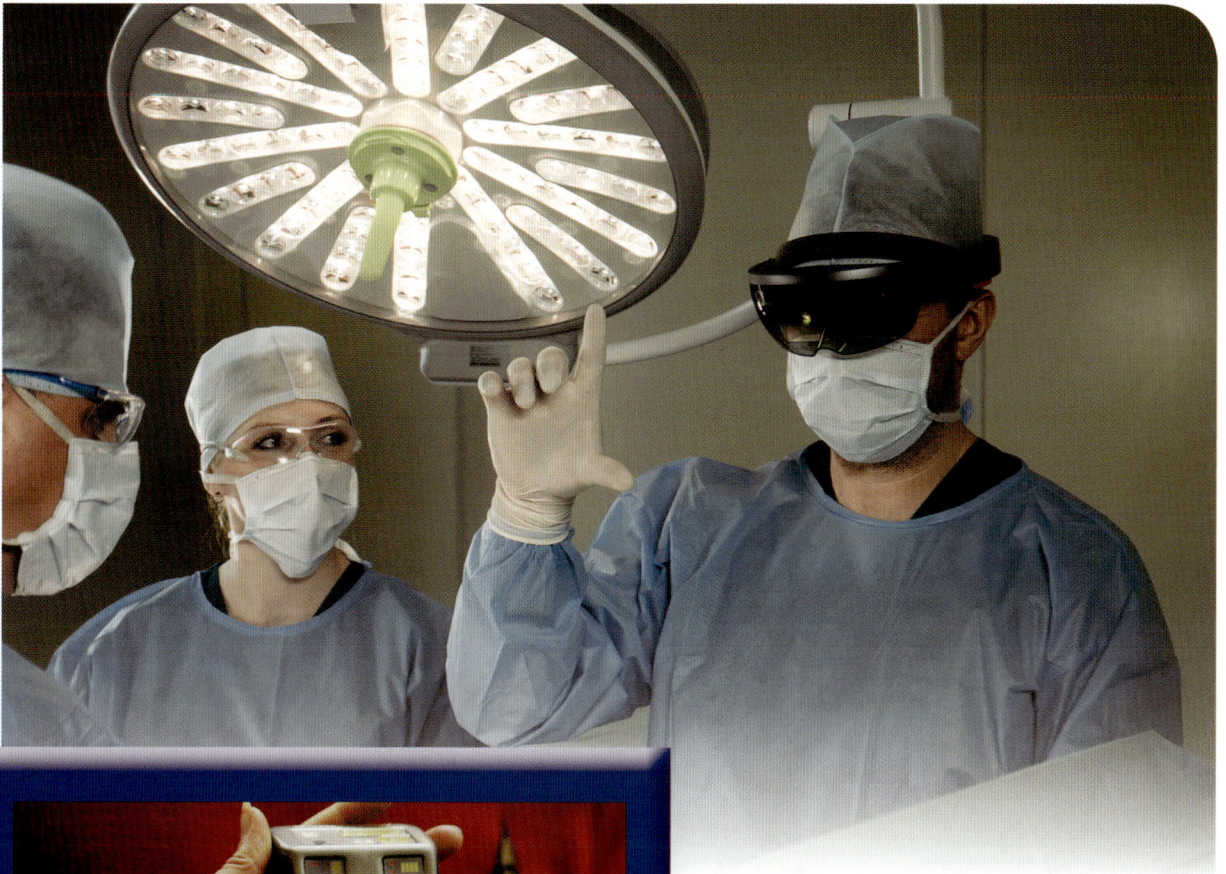

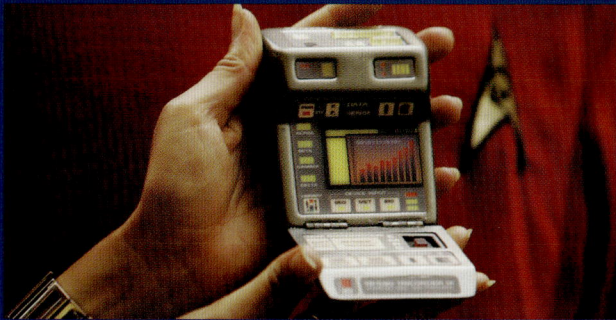

TRICORDER

In the 1960's, the television series "Star Trek" portrayed a vision of a promising future made possible by high technology. The show's frequently used tricorder was a hand-held scanner that could instantly diagnose any medical condition, among other capabilities. Technology enthusiasts have hoped to create a real-life tricorder ever since.

Virtual reality (VR) is an interactive computer-generated experience that takes place in a simulated environment. Once considered mainly a toy, VR is making its way into healthcare. Virtual reality has been incorporated into therapies designed to treat chronic pain and memory loss, among other conditions. Surgeons also use VR to practice complex medical procedures.

6 A NEW SOURCE OF FOOD

LAB TO TABLE

Eating food grown in a lab may sound a little creepy. But lab-grown food could actually improve our lives. In the future, your menu may include several new foods that only exist thanks to high-tech innovations in food production. These technologies may give people better access to fresh food, while reducing our use of precious resources.

Many **nutritionists** consider meat to be an important part of a well-balanced diet. Meat supplies vitamins, minerals, and fat necessary for good health and growth. Meat also provides an especially good source of proteins, which the body needs to build and maintain its cells and tissues.

But many people have concerns about how their meat is raised and produced. Factory farms, where highly mechanized systems are used to raise thousands of **livestock** for slaughter, are considered inhumane and produce great amounts of waste and pollution. In such farms, producers raise the animals in confinement, so that they can more easily be managed. This is especially common for livestock producers raising hogs and poultry, where the animals are kept in a building, never free to roam outside for their entire life.

New technologies are increasingly focused not only on producing enough food to feed a growing population, but also on the welfare of livestock and reducing the waste and pollution of modern factory farming.

A technician works with "meat" created in a laboratory, rather than by raising and slaughtering livestock. Lab-grown meat could give more people the protein they need, while eliminating the waste, pollution, and suffering associated with livestock farming.

MEAT WITHOUT ANIMALS

Would you eat a hamburger that was grown in a lab? Public perception is just one challenge facing **cellular agriculture** and **synthetic** foods. Cellular agriculture is the use of cells to grow farm-product substitutes.

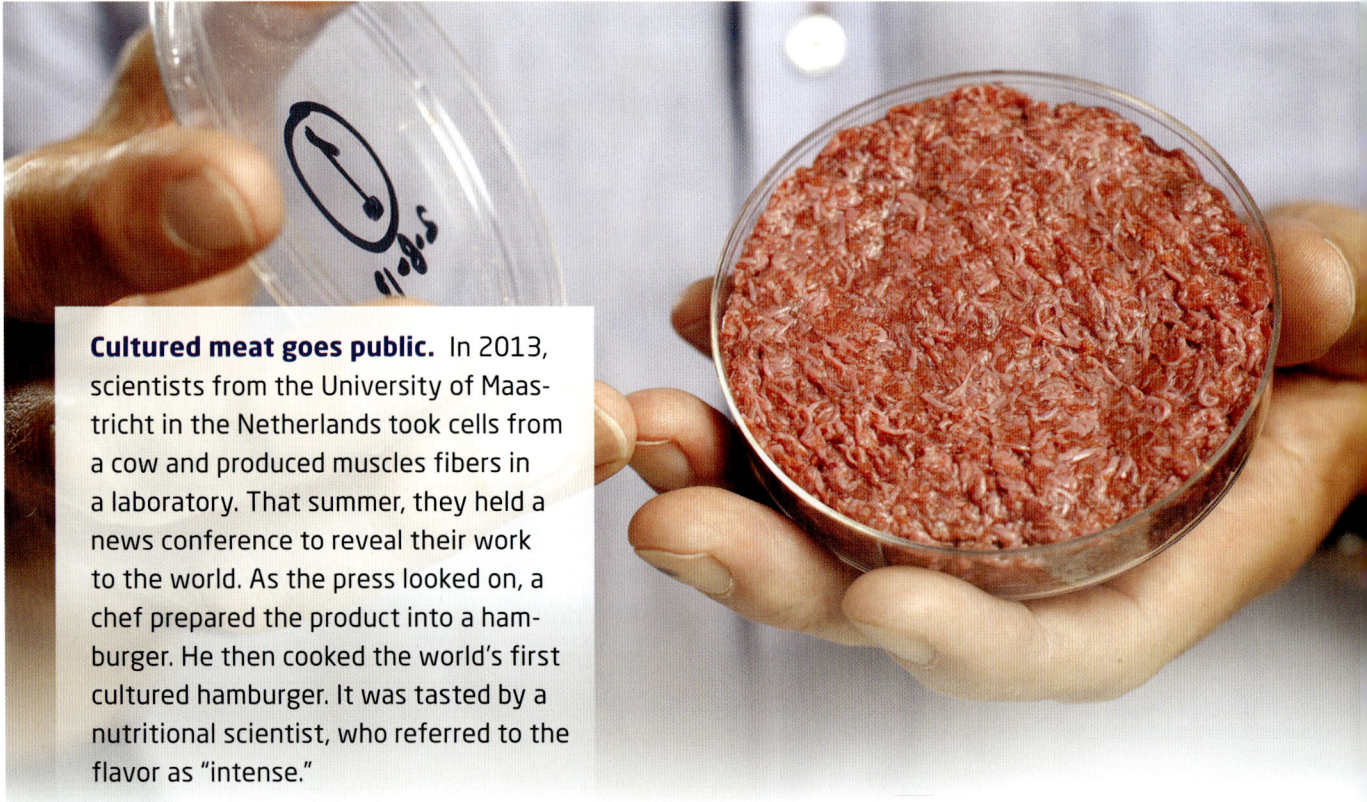

Cultured meat goes public. In 2013, scientists from the University of Maastricht in the Netherlands took cells from a cow and produced muscles fibers in a laboratory. That summer, they held a news conference to reveal their work to the world. As the press looked on, a chef prepared the product into a hamburger. He then cooked the world's first cultured hamburger. It was tasted by a nutritional scientist, who referred to the flavor as "intense."

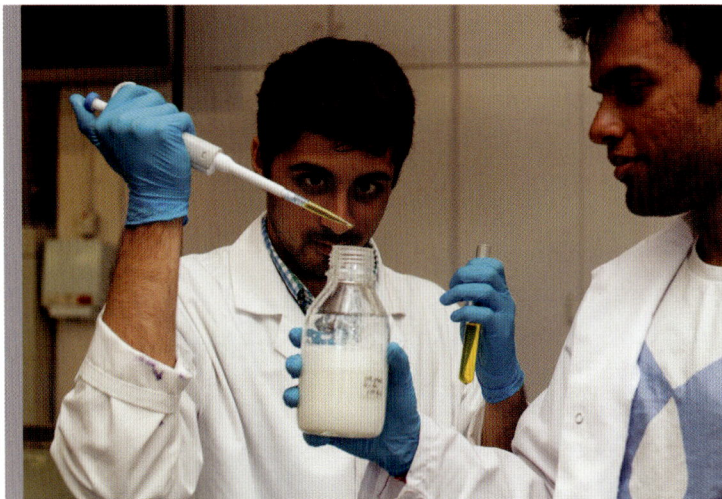

Synthetic foods. New Harvest, a company headquartered in New York City, holds an annual conference on advancements in cellular agriculture. Connecting scientists and business-people, New Harvest has helped to establish companies that produce cellular foods. One of them is Muufri, which is producing animal-free milk. Another is Memphis Meats, which produced the first cellular-grown meatball in 2016.

Cellular agriculture (sometimes shortened to *cell ag*) may replace farm animals. Cellular agriculture is the production of such agricultural products as eggs, milk, and meat from cells grown under controlled conditions in a laboratory.

Regulatory hurdles. One of the most serious concerns facing cellular agriculture is regulation—whose job is it to make sure such foods are safe and nutritious? In the United States, the Department of Agriculture (USDA) oversees animal products such as meat, milk, and eggs. But the U.S. Food and Drug Administration (FDA) is mainly responsible for products made from cell cultures.

> Cellular agriculture has many potential benefits for healthy eating and the environment. But the industry will be successful only if the synthetic foods are appealing and taste good.

Yuck factor. Many people have a negative attitude toward food produced in a laboratory. It just does not seem organic or natural. This may change with time. Jewish and Muslim communities may ask if such foods are acceptable under their strict dietary laws. Other potential obstacles include market competition with more traditional sources of agricultural products.

FARMING THE FUTURE

The future of farming may be cells, not cattle. To overcome the many challenges to cellular agriculture, proponents attempt to explain the process in clear terms to eliminate any mystery surrounding the underlying science of this technology and the manufacturing processes involved. They also emphasize the many positive environmental and ethical benefits of meat without animals.

Raising meat in a lab instead of a pasture will help reduce pollution and free up land for other uses. Today, about one quarter of Earth's farmable land is used to raise livestock. Even more land is used to grow food for livestock to eat.

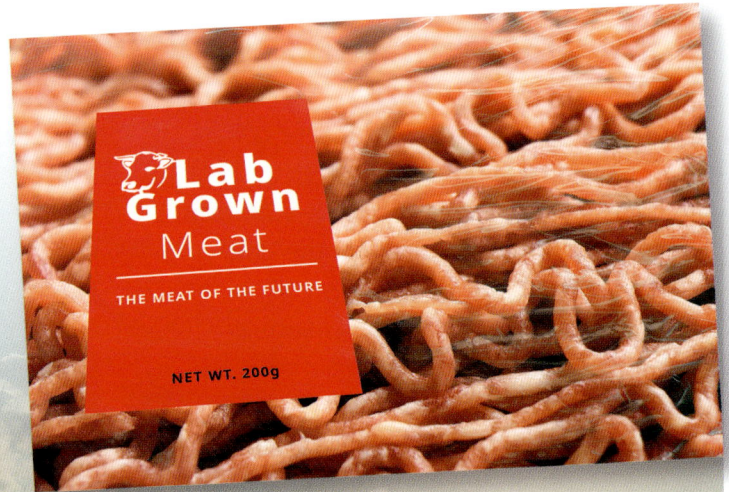

Lab
Grown
Meat
THE MEAT OF THE FUTURE
NET WT. 200g

A more humane world. Many animal welfare groups favor cellular agriculture because it diminishes the need to kill or confine animals to provide food for human beings. These groups see cellular agriculture as a way to establish a more humane world in which farms and slaughterhouses are replaced by laboratories.

Serious savings. Producing milk, meat, and eggs for a growing human population through traditional farming methods is increasingly affecting our environment. Modern livestock facilities are a significant source of greenhouse gases, a cause of climate change. Waste from huge livestock facilities is unsightly, smelly, and threatens to pollute rivers and lakes. Cellular agriculture promises to change all that, producing meat and milk without the animals.

GLOSSARY

avatar an image created on a computer to represent one's role in an internet interaction, such as an online game or conversation.

bionic consisting of electronic or mechanical parts that enhance anatomical structures.

biotechnology the use of living things and life processes to benefit human beings, also called biotech.

calorie a unit of the energy supplied by food.

cellular agriculture the production of such agricultural products as eggs, milk, and meat from cells grown under controlled conditions in a laboratory.

chromosome thin threadlike structure found in cells of all organisms. Chromosomes are the carriers of inheritance—the physical or behavioral characteristics offspring receive from parents.

CRISPR a technology used to "edit" a living thing's DNA by adding, altering, or deleting genes.

DNA deoxyribonucleic acid, a thin, chainlike molecule found in every living cell. It directs the formation, growth, and reproduction of cells and organisms.

donor a living thing from whose body an organ or other part is removed for use.

endangered species living things threatened with extinction—that is, the dying off of all of their kind.

extinct a species that is no longer existing.

futurist a person who studies the future and makes predictions about it based on current trends.

gene a part of a chromosome that influences inheritance and development of some character.

genetic engineering the term applied to techniques that alter the genes or combination of genes in an organism.

livestock domestic animals that are used to produce food and many other valuable products.

nutritionist an expert in the study of nutrition, the processes by which living things take in food and use it.

organ any part of an animal or plant that is composed of various tissues organized to do certain things in life. The eyes, stomach, heart, and lungs are organs of the body.

parasite an animal or plant that lives on or in another from which it gets its food, always at the expense of the host.

rehabilitation the act or process involved to restore the body to good condition.

synthetic made artificially.

transplant (in medicine) surgery that transfers any type of tissue or organ from one person to another. Transplanted tissues and organs replace diseased, damaged, or destroyed body parts.

INDEX

ACKNOWLEDGMENTS

5 © ESB Professional/Shutterstock

6-7 © Gregor Fischer, picture alliance/Getty Images; © Vchal/Shutterstock

8-9 © Lesterman/Shutterstock; Dennis Schroeder, NREL/U.S. Department of Energy; © ESB Professional/Shutterstock; © Helen Sushitskaya, Shutterstock; © DN1988/Shutterstock

10-11 © Chansom Pantip, Shutterstock; © MediaNews Group/Orange County Register/Getty Images

12-13 © Shutterstock

14-15 © Universal Images Group/Getty Images; © Blue Ring Media/Shutterstock

16-17 © Shutterstock

18-19 © ullstein bild/Getty Images; © Spencer Platt, Getty Images; © BSIP/UIG/Getty Images; © Mirko Sobotta, Shutterstock

20-21 © Wang Zhao, AFP/Getty Images; © Alexander Kabanov, Shutterstock

22-23 © Lisa S, Shutterstock; © Designua/Shutterstock; © Enrico Spanu, REDA&CO/UIG/Getty Images; © Toru Yamanaka, AFP/Getty Images

24-25 Cryonics Institute/EPA; © Patrick Landmann, Science Photo Library; © Mistery/Shutterstock; © Phonlamai Photo/Shutterstock

26-27 © Jin Liwang, Xinhua News Agency/Getty Images

28-29 © Karen Kasmauski, Getty Images; © Cameron Watson, Shutterstock; © ESB Professional/Shutterstock

30-31 © Oregon National Primate Research Center; © Tony Gutierrez, AP Photo; © SPUTNIK/Alamy Images; © Gamma-Rapho/Getty Images; © Andrew M. Allport, Shutterstock

32-33 © Gorodenkoff/Shutterstock

34-35 © Elnur/Shutterstock; © Ben Hider, Getty Images; © Olesia Bilkei, Shutterstock; © Zapp 2 Photo/Shutterstock

36-37 © Steve Parsons, PA Images/Getty Images; National Museum of Health and Medicine photo illustration by Matthew Breitbart; © Images Press/Getty Images; © Frederick Florin, AFP/Getty Images; © MCA TV

38-39 X PRIZE; © Supamotion/Shutterstock; © Bruno Vincent, Getty Images

40-41 © Anyaivanova/Shutterstock

42-43 © David Parry, PA Images/Alamy Images; © New Harvest; © FXQuadro/Shutterstock

44-45 © Akarat Phasura, iStockphoto; © Patrick Jennings, Shutterstock; © The Len/Shutterstock; © New Africa/Shutterstock